. tiny book of .

SWEETS &
CONFECTIONS

Small Pleasures
· SERIES ·

hm | books

.tiny book of.
SWEETS &
CONFECTIONS

DECADENT TREATS *for* SPECIAL OCCASIONS

Small Pleasures
· SERIES ·
hm|books

PRESIDENT/CCO *Brian Hart Hoffman*
VICE PRESIDENT/SHELTER CONTENT *Cindy Smith Cooper*
GROUP CREATIVE DIRECTOR *Deanna Rippy Gardner*
ART DIRECTOR *Cristela Tschumy*

EDITORIAL
RECIPE EDITOR *Fran Jensen*
COPY EDITOR *Meg Lundberg*
CREATIVE DIRECTOR/PHOTOGRAPHY *Mac Jamieson*
SENIOR PHOTOGRAPHERS *John O'Hagan,*
Marcy Black Simpson
PHOTOGRAPHERS *Jim Bathie, William Dickey,*
Stephanie Welbourne Steele
ASSISTANT PHOTOGRAPHER *Caroline Smith*
SENIOR DIGITAL IMAGING SPECIALIST *Delisa McDaniel*
DIGITAL IMAGING SPECIALIST *Clark Densmore*
STYLISTS *Sidney Bragiel, Lucy Herndon,*
Yukie McLean, Tracey Runnion
FOOD STYLISTS AND RECIPE DEVELOPERS *Laura Crandall,*
Melissa Gray, Kathleen Kanen, Nancy Hughes,
Vanessa Rocchio, Elizabeth Stringer, Emily Turner
ASSISTANT FOOD STYLIST/RECIPE DEVELOPER *Anita Simpson Spain*

CHAIRMAN OF THE BOARD/CEO *Phyllis Hoffman DePiano*
PRESIDENT/COO *Eric W. Hoffman*
PRESIDENT/CCO *Brian Hart Hoffman*
EXECUTIVE VICE PRESIDENT/CFO *Mary P. Cummings*
EXECUTIVE VICE PRESIDENT/O&M *Greg Baugh*
VICE PRESIDENT/DIGITAL MEDIA *Jon Adamson*
VICE PRESIDENT/CULINARY/CUSTOM CONTENT *Brooke Michael Bell*
VICE PRESIDENT/SHELTER CONTENT *Cindy Smith Cooper*
VICE PRESIDENT/ADMINISTRATION *Lynn Lee Terry*

Hoffman Media
1900 International Park Drive, Suite 50
Birmingham, Alabama 35243
www.hoffmanmedia.com
ISBN # 978-0-9785489-0-2
Printed in China

ON THE COVER:
(Front) Hummingbird Cake Truffles and
Chocolate-Bourbon Truffles, page 63.
(Back) White Chocolate Cranberry Toffee 122.

.contents.

introduction.

No matter the season, there's always room for sweets on the table.

FROM HOLIDAYS TO BIRTHDAY PARTIES TO A TYPICAL WEEKDAY AFTERNOON, any day is made more charming and special with a confection. Whether you love truffles, fudge, cake bites, bonbons, or bark, The *Tiny Book of Sweets & Confections* is bursting with dozens of recipes to satisfy any sweet tooth. Whether Cookies and Cream Truffles or Bridge Mix Clusters, each decadent treat is doable for even the novice confectioner.

Most sweets and confections are a breeze to make, especially with our easy-to-follow directions. This book is divided into three sections: Sweet Bites, Sweet Confections, and Sweet Treats. Within each recipe, you will find techniques, details about the ingredients, and ideas for presenting them for gifts, too. All of the recipes in this book are tested in our test kitchens and are sure to become some of your favorites.

So, tie on an apron, grab the sugar, and dive into The *Tiny Book of Sweets & Confections* in the kitchen.

— Cindy

Sweet Bites

MEMORIES ARE MADE WITH THESE
SPECIAL RECIPES TO SHARE
OR TAKE ALONG.

Salted Caramel Macaroons

MAKES ABOUT 24

1 (14-ounce) bag
    sweetened flaked
    coconut
1 cup chopped pecans
¾ cup sweetened
    condensed milk
¾ cup Salted Caramel
    Sauce (recipe follows)
1 large egg white, lightly
    beaten
2 teaspoons vanilla
    extract
¼ teaspoon kosher salt
1 (12-ounce) package
    semisweet chocolate
    morsels, melted
Garnish: Salted Caramel
    Sauce

SALTED CARAMEL SAUCE

MAKES ABOUT 1 CUP

1 cup sugar
¼ cup water
½ cup unsalted butter,
    softened
½ cup heavy whipping
    cream, room
    temperature
½ teaspoon kosher salt

Preheat oven to 325°. Line baking sheets with parchment paper.

In a large bowl, stir together coconut, pecans, condensed milk, Salted Caramel Sauce, egg white, vanilla, and salt until combined. Using a 1-inch spring-loaded ice cream scoop, scoop coconut mixture into mounds, and place at least 2 inches apart on prepared pans.

Bake until tops are lightly browned, 15 to 17 minutes. Let cool completely on pans.

Dip bottom of each cooled macaroon into melted chocolate; return to pan. Refrigerate until chocolate hardens, about 15 minutes. Drizzle with remaining Salted Caramel Sauce, if desired. Store in airtight containers for up to 3 days.

SALTED CARAMEL SAUCE
In a medium saucepan, bring sugar and ¼ cup water to a boil over medium heat. Cook, without stirring, until mixture is amber colored. (Brush sides of pan with water to prevent caramel from crystallizing.) Remove from heat; stir in butter, cream, and salt. (Mixture will boil vigorously.) Let cool to room temperature before using.

Kitchen TIP

The Salted Caramel Sauce can be made ahead and refrigerated for up to 1 week.

Lemon-Ginger Cake Bites

Preheat oven to 350°. Spray a 9-inch square baking pan with baking spray with flour.

In a large bowl, beat butter and sugar with a mixer at medium speed until fluffy, 3 to 4 minutes, stopping to scrape sides of bowl. Add eggs, one at a time, beating well after each addition. Beat in vanilla.

In a medium bowl, whisk together flour, baking powder, ground ginger, and salt. With mixer on low speed, gradually add flour mixture to butter mixture alternately with milk, beginning and ending with flour mixture, beating just until combined after each addition. Stir in crystallized ginger. Spoon batter into prepared pan.

Bake until a wooden pick inserted in center comes out clean, 40 to 50 minutes. Let cool in pan for 10 minutes. Remove from pan, and let cool completely on a wire rack.

In a large bowl, crumble cake. Add lemon curd, and beat with a mixer at medium speed until combined.

Line baking sheets with parchment paper. Roll cake mixture into 1-inch balls. Dip cake balls in melted candy coating, and place on prepared pans. Garnish with crystallized ginger, if desired. Let stand until set, about 15 minutes. Cover and refrigerate for up to 3 days.

MAKES ABOUT 60

½ cup unsalted butter, softened
1¾ cups sugar
3 large eggs
1 teaspoon vanilla extract
2½ cups all-purpose flour
2½ teaspoons baking powder
1 teaspoon ground ginger
¼ teaspoon salt
1 cup whole milk
½ cup chopped crystallized ginger
1 (10-ounce) jar lemon curd
1½ (16-ounce) packages vanilla-flavored candy coating, melted according to package directions
Garnish: finely chopped crystallized ginger

Coconut Cake Bites

1 (15.25-ounce) box
    white cake mix
2 cups sweetened flaked
    coconut, divided
1 cup coconut milk
⅓ cup coconut oil,
    melted
3 large eggs
4 ounces cream cheese,
    softened
½ cup heavy whipping
    cream
2 tablespoons
    confectioners' sugar
Cream Cheese Fondant
    (recipe follows)
30 wooden lollipop
    sticks

CREAM CHEESE FONDANT
Makes about 2½ cups

4 ounces cream cheese,
    softened
¼ cup heavy whipping
    cream
¼ cup light corn syrup
1 teaspoon coconut
    extract
4 cups confectioners'
    sugar

Preheat oven to 350°. Spray a 13x9-inch baking pan with baking spray with flour.

In a large bowl, beat cake mix, 1 cup coconut, coconut milk, melted coconut oil, and eggs with a mixer at medium-high speed until combined. Spread in prepared pan.

Bake until a wooden pick inserted in center comes out clean, about 30 minutes. Let cool completely.

In a medium bowl, beat cream cheese, cream, confectioners' sugar, and remaining 1 cup coconut with a mixer at high speed until smooth. Crumble cooled cake over cream cheese mixture, and beat at medium speed until combined.

Line a rimmed baking sheet with parchment paper; top with a wire rack. Roll cake mixture into 1-inch balls, and place on prepared rack. Cover and refrigerate for 30 minutes.

Pour Cream Cheese Fondant over cake balls to coat, letting excess drip off. Let stand until fondant is set. Drizzle with remaining Cream Cheese Fondant as desired. Insert a lollipop stick into top of each cake bite before serving. Cover and refrigerate for up to 3 days.

CREAM CHEESE FONDANT
In the top of a double boiler, combine cream cheese, cream, corn syrup, and coconut extract. Cook over simmering water, stirring occasionally, until mixture is smooth. Whisk in confectioners' sugar, 1 cup at a time, until mixture is smooth. Use immediately.

Bourbon Balls

Preheat oven to 350°. Spray a large rimmed baking sheet with baking spray with flour.

In a small microwave-safe bowl, microwave butter and chocolate on high in 30-second intervals, stirring between each, until melted and smooth.

In a large bowl, whisk together eggs, brown sugar, vanilla, and salt. Add chocolate mixture, whisking until smooth.

In a medium bowl, whisk together flour, cinnamon, and anise. Add flour mixture to egg mixture, stirring until combined. Pour batter into prepared pan, smoothing top with an offset spatula.

Bake until a wooden pick inserted in center comes out with some crumbs attached, 7 to 9 minutes. Let cool in pan on a wire rack. Break into 1-inch pieces.

Transfer pieces to the bowl of a stand mixer fitted with the paddle attachment. With mixer on low speed, add bourbon and orange zest and juice, beating until mixture comes together and forms a ball.

Using a tablespoon, scoop dough, and shape into 1-inch balls. Roll in turbinado sugar to coat. Refrigerate for 2 hours. Serve chilled or at room temperature. Cover and refrigerate for up to 1 week.

MAKES ABOUT 36

- ¾ cup unsalted butter, cubed
- 6 ounces semisweet chocolate, finely chopped
- 3 large eggs
- ½ cup firmly packed light brown sugar
- 1 teaspoon vanilla extract
- ½ teaspoon kosher salt
- ¾ cup all-purpose flour
- ½ teaspoon ground cinnamon
- ¼ teaspoon ground anise
- ¼ cup bourbon
- ½ teaspoon orange zest
- 1 tablespoon fresh orange juice
- ½ cup turbinado sugar

Mini Pumpkin Whoopie Pies

¾ cup canned pumpkin
½ cup granulated sugar
½ cup firmly packed light
   brown sugar
½ cup canola oil
1 large egg, lightly beaten
½ teaspoon vanilla extract
1½ cups all-purpose flour
1 tablespoon pumpkin pie
   spice
½ teaspoon salt
½ teaspoon baking powder
½ teaspoon baking soda
Buttered Rum–
   Marshmallow Filling
   (recipe follows)
Garnish: toffee bits

BUTTERED RUM–MARSHMALLOW FILLING
Makes about 1½ cups

¼ cup butter, softened
3 ounces cream cheese,
   softened
½ cup confectioners' sugar
¼ teaspoon butter
   flavoring
¼ teaspoon rum extract
¼ teaspoon vanilla extract

Preheat oven to 350°. Line 2 baking sheets with parchment paper.

In a large bowl, combine pumpkin, sugars, oil, egg, and vanilla. In a medium bowl, whisk together flour, pumpkin pie spice, salt, baking powder, and baking soda. Add flour mixture to pumpkin mixture, whisking to combine.

Using a 1-inch spring-loaded ice cream scoop, scoop dough, and place at least 2 inches apart on prepared pans.

Bake until puffed and edges are lightly browned, 10 to 12 minutes. Let cool on pans for 10 minutes. Remove from pans, and let cool completely on wire racks.

Spread about 2 teaspoons Buttered Rum–Marshmallow Filling onto flat side of half of cookies. Place remaining cookies, flat side down, on top of filling. Sprinkle edges with toffee bits, if desired. Refrigerate in an airtight container for up to 5 days.

BUTTERED RUM–MARSHMALLOW FILLING
In a medium bowl, beat butter and cream cheese with a mixer at medium-high speed until smooth and creamy, about 3 minutes. Add confectioners' sugar, flavoring, and extracts, beating until combined. Refrigerate until ready to use.

Triple Chocolate Cake Bites

Preheat oven to 350°. Spray a 13x9-inch baking pan with baking spray with flour.

In a large bowl, stir together cake mix and cocoa. Add ¾ cup water, oil, and eggs; beat with a mixer at medium speed until smooth. Stir in sour cream. Spoon mixture into prepared pan.

Bake until a wooden pick inserted in center comes out clean, about 25 minutes. Let cool completely in pan. In a large bowl, crumble cake.

In a small saucepan, combine chopped chocolate and cream. Cook over low heat, stirring frequently, until chocolate is melted and smooth. Stir in preserves. Spoon mixture over crumbled cake, and beat with a mixer at medium speed until combined.

Line 2 baking sheets with parchment paper. Roll cake mixture into 1-inch balls, and place on prepared pans. Cover and freeze for at least 1 hour or up to 1 month. Using 2 forks, dip cake balls in melted candy coating, shaking off excess. Return to pans, and let stand until set, about 10 minutes. Drizzle with melted white chocolate. Cover and refrigerate for up to 3 days.

MAKES ABOUT 48

- 1 (15.25-ounce) box devil's food cake mix
- 2 tablespoons unsweetened cocoa powder
- ¾ cup water
- ½ cup vegetable oil
- 3 large eggs
- ½ cup sour cream
- 2 (4-ounce) bars semisweet chocolate, chopped
- ¼ cup heavy whipping cream
- ¼ cup seedless raspberry preserves
- 2 (16-ounce) packages chocolate-flavored candy coating, melted according to package directions
- 1 (4-ounce) bar white chocolate, melted

Frozen Cake Batter Bonbons

1 (8-ounce) package
   cream cheese,
   softened
½ cup butter, softened
1 (18.25-ounce) box
   white cake mix
3 tablespoons
   strawberry extract
2 (16-ounce) packages
   vanilla-flavored
   candy coating, melted
   according to package
   directions
Garnish: pink and white
   jimmies

In a large bowl, beat cream cheese and butter with a mixer at medium speed until creamy. Add cake mix and strawberry extract, beating to combine. Cover and freeze for 2 hours.

Line 2 baking sheets with parchment paper. Roll cream cheese mixture into 1-inch balls, and place on prepared pans.

Using 2 forks, dip cake balls in melted candy coating, letting excess drip off. Return to pans, and sprinkle with jimmies, if desired. Return to freezer. Serve frozen. Freeze in an airtight container for up to 2 weeks.

Banana Beignets with Maple Glaze

In a large Dutch oven, pour oil to a depth of 2 inches, and heat over medium-high heat until a deep-fry thermometer registers 350°.

In a large bowl, whisk together flour, ½ cup sugar, baking powder, 1 teaspoon cinnamon, baking soda, and salt. In a medium bowl, combine milk, banana, egg, banana extract, and remaining 2 tablespoons oil. Add milk mixture to flour mixture, stirring just until combined.

Working in batches, drop dough by tablespoonfuls into hot oil, and fry until golden brown, about 2 minutes. Remove beignets from oil using a slotted spoon, and let drain on a wire rack with paper towels underneath.

In a shallow bowl, combine remaining ½ cup sugar and remaining ½ teaspoon cinnamon. While beignets are still warm, roll in cinnamon sugar mixture. Drizzle with Maple Glaze.

MAPLE GLAZE
In a small bowl, whisk together confectioners' sugar and maple syrup until smooth.

MAKES ABOUT 5 SERVINGS

2 tablespoons vegetable oil, plus more for frying
2 cups cake flour
1 cup sugar, divided
1½ teaspoons baking powder
1½ teaspoons ground cinnamon, divided
½ teaspoon baking soda
½ teaspoon salt
½ cup whole milk
½ cup mashed banana (about 1 large banana)
1 large egg
¼ teaspoon banana extract
Maple Glaze (recipe follows)

MAPLE GLAZE
MAKES ABOUT ½ CUP

1 cup confectioners' sugar
½ cup pure maple syrup

Apricot-Date Snowballs

1 cup granulated sugar
½ cup whole pitted
 dates, chopped
½ cup dried apricots,
 chopped
½ cup unsalted butter
¼ teaspoon kosher salt
1 large egg
2 cups crisp rice cereal*
½ cup chopped toasted
 pecans
½ teaspoon vanilla
 extract
1 cup confectioners'
 sugar
1 cup sweetened flaked
 coconut

In a large saucepan, stir together granulated sugar, dates, apricots, butter, salt, and egg. Bring to a simmer over medium heat, stirring frequently to prevent scorching. Reduce heat, and simmer, stirring frequently, until thickened and golden brown, about 10 minutes. Remove from heat. Stir in cereal, pecans, and vanilla. Let stand until cool enough to handle. (Mixture should still be slightly warm.)

Line a large baking sheet with parchment paper. Shape mixture into 1-inch balls. Roll in confectioners' sugar or coconut, and place on prepared pan. Let stand until cool. Store in an airtight container.

We used Kellogg's Rice Krispies Cereal.

Cottontails

Preheat oven to 400°. Line baking sheets with parchment paper.

In a medium saucepan, bring 1 cup water and butter to a boil over medium heat. Add flour and salt, stirring vigorously with a wooden spoon until mixture forms a ball. Remove from heat; let cool for 10 minutes.

Add eggs, one at a time, beating with a wooden spoon after each addition until smooth, about 30 seconds. Spoon or pipe mixture into 1½-inch mounds 2 inches apart onto prepared pans.

Bake until golden and puffy, 25 to 30 minutes. Let cool on a wire rack.

Cut off top of each cream puff, reserving tops; pull out and discard soft dough inside. Drizzle reserved tops of cream puffs with melted candy coating, and sprinkle with coconut. Let stand until set. Spoon or pipe Cottontail Cream into bottoms of cream puffs. Place prepared tops over cream. Refrigerate until ready to serve.

COTTONTAIL CREAM

In a small bowl, beat cream cheese, sour cream, and pudding mix with a mixer at medium speed until smooth. Increase mixer speed to high. Add cream and confectioners' sugar, beating until fluffy. Cover and refrigerate for 30 minutes.

MAKES ABOUT 48

1 cup water
½ cup unsalted butter
1 cup all-purpose flour
¼ teaspoon salt
4 large eggs
1 (16-ounce) package vanilla-flavored candy coating, melted according to package directions
1 (14-ounce) bag sweetened flaked coconut
Cottontail Cream (recipe follows)

COTTONTAIL CREAM
MAKES ABOUT 3½ CUPS

1 (8-ounce) package cream cheese, softened
¾ cup sour cream
1 (3.4-ounce) box vanilla instant pudding mix
2 cups heavy whipping cream
½ cup confectioners' sugar

Tropical Coconut Macaroons

MAKES ABOUT 48

**2 (14-ounce) bags
   sweetened flaked
   coconut**
1 cup sugar
½ cup all-purpose flour
½ teaspoon salt
8 egg whites
**½ cup finely chopped
   salted macadamia
   nuts**
**½ cup finely chopped
   dried pineapple**
**½ cup finely chopped
   dried mango**

Preheat oven to 325°. Line baking sheets with parchment paper.

In a large bowl, beat coconut, sugar, flour, and salt with a mixer at medium speed until combined. Add egg whites, beating until combined. Stir in nuts, pineapple, and mango. Drop dough by rounded tablespoonfuls 2 inches apart onto prepared pans.

Bake until edges are lightly browned, 18 to 20 minutes. Let cool on pans for 2 minutes. Remove from pans, and let cool completely on wire racks.

Peppermint Macaroons

Preheat oven to 300°. Line baking sheets with parchment paper.

In a large bowl, whisk together egg whites and salt until foamy, about 2 minutes. Whisk in condensed milk and vanilla. Stir in coconut, chocolate morsels, and peppermints. Using a 1½-inch spring-loaded scoop, scoop dough onto prepared pans.

Bake until lightly browned, about 20 minutes. Let cool on pans for 10 minutes. Remove from pans, and let cool completely on wire racks. Store in an airtight container for up to 3 days.

MAKES ABOUT 30

2 egg whites, room temperature
⅛ teaspoon salt
1 (14-ounce) can sweetened condensed milk
1 teaspoon vanilla extract
2 (14-ounce) packages sweetened flaked coconut
1 cup white chocolate morsels
½ cup crushed peppermint candies

Forget-Me-Not Cookies

MAKES ABOUT 60

6 large egg whites, room temperature
1½ cups sugar
1 cup chocolate-covered toffee bits
1 cup finely chopped toasted pecans

Preheat oven to 350°. Line baking sheets with parchment paper.

In a large bowl, beat egg whites with a mixer at high speed until soft peaks form. Gradually add sugar, beating until stiff peaks form. Gently fold in toffee bits and pecans. Drop by rounded tablespoonfuls onto prepared pans.

Place cookies in oven. Turn oven off, and let meringues stand in oven with door closed for at least 8 hours or overnight.

Kitchen TIP

Multiple oven racks can be used at one time. To make round, uniform cookies, use a 1-tablespoon cookie scoop.

Homemade Peppermint Patties

Line a 13x9-inch baking pan with foil, letting excess extend over sides of pan.

In a medium saucepan, bring sugar, butter, milk, and salt to a boil over high heat, whisking frequently. Reduce heat to medium. Cook, stirring constantly, until mixture registers 234° on a candy thermometer. Remove from heat; stir in white chocolate, marshmallow crème, and 1 cup peppermints. Spread into prepared pan. Freeze for 2 hours.

Using excess foil as handles, remove from pan. Using a 2½-inch round cutter, cut into rounds. Line a baking sheet with parchment paper. Using 2 forks, dip rounds in melted chocolate, coating completely. Place on prepared pan. Sprinkle with remaining ¼ cup peppermints. Let stand for 1 hour. Cover and refrigerate for up to 1 week.

MAKES ABOUT 48

- 2 cups sugar
- ¾ cup unsalted butter
- ⅔ cup whole milk
- ¼ teaspoon salt
- 3 (4-ounce) bars white chocolate, chopped
- 1 (7-ounce) jar marshmallow crème
- 1¼ cups finely chopped soft peppermints, divided
- 3 (4-ounce) bars bittersweet chocolate, melted

Caramel Cake Bites

MAKES 24

**2 (16-ounce) packages
frozen pound cake,
thawed**
**1 (11-ounce) package
caramel bits**
**3 tablespoons heavy
whipping cream**
**1 (12-ounce) package
white chocolate
morsels**
¾ cup cookie butter*
**½ cup all-vegetable
shortening**
**Caramel Brittle (recipe
follows)**

CARAMEL BRITTLE
MAKES ABOUT 4 CUPS

2 cups sugar
1 cup water

Using a serrated knife, remove crusts from cake; discard. Trim each cake into an 8¾x3½-inch rectangle. Cut each cake in half lengthwise.

In a small saucepan, combine caramel bits and cream. Cook over medium-low heat, whisking constantly, until mixture is smooth. Remove from heat, and let cool until mixture is a spreadable consistency.

Spread a thin layer of caramel mixture onto 2 cake layers. Top each with remaining cake layers. Wrap each cake in heavy-duty plastic wrap, and freeze for at least 2 hours or up to 1 month.

Line a rimmed baking sheet with parchment paper; top with a wire rack.

Unwrap cakes, trimming excess caramel if necessary. Cut each cake into 12 portions. Place cakes on prepared rack.

In a microwave-safe bowl, combine white chocolate morsels, cookie butter, and shortening. Microwave on high in 30-second intervals, stirring between each, until mixture is melted and smooth. Spoon mixture over cakes. Using a spatula, spread and smooth frosting over cakes. Let stand until frosting is set, about 30 minutes. Top each with Caramel Brittle. Cover and refrigerate for up to 3 days.

We used Biscoff Cookie Butter.

CARAMEL BRITTLE
Line a rimmed baking sheet with a silicone baking mat.
In a large saucepan, bring sugar and 1 cup water to a boil over medium-high heat. Cook until mixture registers 360° on a candy thermometer. Immediately pour mixture onto prepared pan. Let stand until mixture hardens, about 30 minutes. Break into pieces. Freeze in an airtight container for up to 5 days.

Pistachio-Cherry Nougat Bites

Line a 9-inch square baking pan with foil, letting excess extend over sides of pan. Spray with cooking spray.

In a large saucepan, combine sugar, honey, and ¾ cup water. Cook over medium heat until mixture registers 260° on a candy thermometer.

Meanwhile, in a large bowl, beat egg whites and vanilla bean seeds with a mixer at high speed until stiff peaks form. With mixer on low speed, gradually add hot sugar mixture to egg whites, beating until combined. Add extracts; increase mixer speed to medium-high, and beat for 12 minutes. Add pistachios and cherries; beat for 3 minutes. Spread mixture into prepared pan. Top with almonds, pressing gently. Let stand for 8 hours.

Using excess foil as handles, remove from pan, and cut into 2-inch squares. Store in an airtight container for up to 5 days.

MAKES ABOUT 18

- 3 cups superfine sugar
- ¾ cup honey
- ¾ cup water
- 3 large egg whites
- ½ vanilla bean, split lengthwise, seeds scraped and reserved
- 2 teaspoons vanilla extract
- 1 teaspoon almond extract
- 1½ cups pistachios, coarsely chopped
- ½ cup candied cherries, chopped
- ½ cup toasted sliced almonds

Brownie Petit Fours

MAKES 12

1 (11-ounce) container
    brownie bites
¼ cup creamy peanut
    butter
1 cup dark melting
    wafers*, melted
    according to package
    directions
1 tablespoon heavy
    whipping cream
1 (8-ounce) package
    roasted salted
    peanuts, finely
    chopped

Using the end of a wooden spoon, poke a hole in center of each brownie bite, being careful not to poke all the way through.

Fill a piping bag with peanut butter, and fill each hole with peanut butter. Turn brownie bites over, and place on a wire rack.

In a small bowl, stir together melted chocolate and cream. Pour over brownies. Let cool slightly. Top each brownie with peanuts while still sticky. Refrigerate until set.

We used Ghirardelli.

Chocolate Peanut-Butter Bites

Line an 8x8x2-inch pan with plastic wrap. Set aside.

In the top half of a double boiler, melt candy coating, crunchy peanut butter, and chocolate hazelnut spread over simmering water. Spread chocolate mixture in prepared pan.

In a small saucepan, heat creamy peanut butter over medium-low heat until melted, approximately 8 minutes. Pour over chocolate mixture. Using a table knife, swirl to combine.

Refrigerate until set, approximately 4 hours. Once set, remove chocolate from pan onto a cutting board. Peel away plastic wrap. Using a knife, cut into 2-inch squares. Cut diagonally into triangles.

MAKES 72

- 1 (16-ounce) package choclate flavored candy coating
- 1 cup crunchy peanut butter
- ½ cup cocolate hazelnut spread, such as Nutella
- ¾ cup creamy peanut butter

Sweet Confections

FANCY AND ELEGANT, THESE RECIPES
ADD DELIGHT TO ANY AFFAIR OR
PARTY MENU.

Rum-Cinnamon Caramels

Spray an 8-inch square baking pan with cooking spray. Line pan with parchment paper, letting excess extend over sides of pan.

In a large saucepan, bring 1 cup cream, corn syrup, sugars, and butter to a boil over medium heat, stirring frequently. Add remaining 1 cup cream, stirring to combine. Cook, without stirring, until mixture registers 250° on a candy thermometer. Remove from heat; add extracts, stirring to combine. Pour into prepared pan. Refrigerate overnight.

Let caramel come to room temperature. Using excess parchment as handles, remove from pan, and cut into squares. Wrap caramels in wax paper. Store at room temperature for up to 5 days.

MAKES ABOUT 48

2 cups heavy whipping cream, divided
1½ cups light corn syrup
1 cup granulated sugar
1 cup firmly packed light brown sugar
1 cup butter
½ teaspoon rum extract
½ teaspoon cinnamon extract

Cookies and Cream Truffles

MAKES ABOUT 24

2 (8-ounce) packages cream cheese, softened
¼ cup confectioners' sugar
1 cup cream-filled chocolate sandwich cookie crumbs (about 10 crushed cookies)
1 (16-ounce) package vanilla-flavored candy coating, melted according to package directions
Garnish: cream-filled chocolate sandwich cookie crumbs

In a medium bowl, beat cream cheese and confectioners' sugar with a mixer at medium speed until creamy. Add cookie crumbs, beating to combine. Cover and refrigerate for 2 hours.

Line baking sheets with parchment papers.

Roll cream cheese mixture into 1-inch balls, and place on prepared pans. Freeze for at least 4 hours or overnight.

Using wooden picks, dip each ball in melted candy coating. Garnish with cookie crumbs, if desired.

Bridge Mix Clusters

In a medium bowl, combine macadamia nuts, cashews, raisins, and toffee bits. Add melted semisweet chocolate, stirring to coat nut mixture completely. Drop by teaspoonfuls onto parchment paper. Drizzle with melted white chocolate. Sprinkle with crushed pretzels. Let stand until set completely.

MAKES ABOUT 84

1 (12-ounce) can macadamia nuts, coarsely chopped
1 (9.75-ounce) can salted cashews, coarsely chopped
½ (15-ounce) box raisins
1 (8-ounce) package chocolate-covered toffee bits
1 (24-ounce) package semisweet chocolate morsels, melted
Melted white chocolate
Crushed pretzels

Kitchen TIP

These can be frozen and thawed in batches for weekly parties. Also, consider using a 1-teaspoon cookie scoop to make the clusters appear more like truffles.

Chocolate-Coconut Drops

MAKES ABOUT 36

½ cup unsalted butter,
   softened
1 cup sugar
2 large eggs
1 teaspoon vanilla
   extract
2 cups all-purpose flour
½ cup unsweetened
   cocoa powder
1 teaspoon baking
   powder
½ teaspoon salt
1¼ cups bittersweet
   chocolate morsels
2 cups sweetened flaked
   coconut

Preheat oven to 350°. Line a large rimmed baking sheet with parchment paper.

In the bowl of a stand mixer fitted with the paddle attachment, beat butter and sugar at medium speed until fluffy, 3 to 4 minutes, stopping to scrape sides of bowl. Add eggs, one at a time, beating well after each addition. Beat in vanilla.

In a medium bowl, whisk together flour, cocoa, baking powder, and salt. With mixer on low speed, gradually add flour mixture to butter mixture, beating until well combined. Add chocolate morsels, beating until combined. (Dough will be thick.)

Place coconut in a medium bowl. Roll dough into 1-inch balls; gently roll each ball in coconut. Place 2 inches apart on prepared pan.

Bake until coconut is lightly toasted and cookies are almost set, about 12 minutes. Let cool on pan for 5 minutes. Remove from pan, and let cool completely on a wire rack. Store in an airtight container for up to 4 days.

Kitchen TIP

After rolling in coconut, place balls on a parchment-lined baking sheet, and freeze until firm. Place balls in a heavy-duty resealable bag, and freeze for up to 1 month. Bake as directed. No thawing necessary.

A Trio of Truffles

In a small bowl, place peanut butter and 1½ tablespoons peanuts. In a second small bowl, place chocolate-hazelnut spread and 1½ tablespoons hazelnuts. In a third small bowl, place cookie spread and 4 chopped cookies.

In a small saucepan, heat cream over medium heat just until bubbles form around edges of pan (do not boil). Remove from heat, and whisk in 1¾ cups chocolate morsels until melted and smooth. Divide chocolate mixture among small bowls; stir each until well combined. Cover bowls, and refrigerate until set, about 2 hours.

Line baking sheets with wax paper. Using a 1½-inch spring-loaded ice cream scoop, scoop chocolate mixture from each bowl into balls, and place on prepared pans, keeping batches separate. Refrigerate for 30 minutes.

In the top of a double boiler, heat oil and remaining 1¼ cups chocolate morsels over simmering water, stirring frequently, until melted and smooth. Using 2 forks, dip balls in melted chocolate to coat, gently tapping off excess. Place on prepared pans, keeping batches separate. Sprinkle batches with remaining ½ tablespoon peanuts, remaining ½ tablespoon hazelnuts, and remaining 2 chopped cookies. Let stand until chocolate is set, about 10 minutes. Refrigerate in an airtight container for up to 3 days.

We used Nutella and Biscoff.

MAKES ABOUT 24

¼ cup creamy peanut butter
2 tablespoons roasted peanuts, finely chopped and divided
¼ cup chocolate-hazelnut spread*
2 tablespoons toasted hazelnuts, finely chopped and divided
¼ cup creamy cookie spread*
6 Biscoff cookies, finely chopped and divided
⅓ cup heavy whipping cream
3 cups semisweet chocolate morsels, divided
2 tablespoons vegetable oil

Chocolate-Covered Crispy Peanut Butter Balls

MAKES ABOUT 36

**1 cup creamy peanut
    butter**
**¼ cup unsalted butter,
    softened**
**2 cups confectioners'
    sugar**
2 cups crisp rice cereal*
**1 (16-ounce)
    package chocolate-
    flavored candy
    coating, melted
    according to package
    directions**
**¼ cup finely chopped
    roasted salted
    peanuts**

In a large bowl, beat peanut butter and butter with a mixer at medium speed until smooth. Gradually beat in confectioners' sugar; stir in cereal. Roll mixture into 1-inch balls. (Refrigerate to prevent mixture from sticking to hands, if needed.)

Line a large baking sheet with wax paper. Using 2 forks, dip each ball in melted candy coating, letting excess drip off. Place on prepared pan; sprinkle with peanuts. Let stand until coating is firm, about 20 minutes. Gently remove from wax paper. Store in an airtight container for up to 1 week.

*We used Kellogg's Rice Krispies Cereal.

Hummingbird Cake Truf

In a medium microwave-safe bowl, combine chocolate morsels, butter, and cream. Microwave on medium in 1-minute intervals, stirring between each, until almost melted (about 2 minutes total). Whisk until mixture is completely smooth. Stir in pecans and pineapple. Pour into a 9-inch pie plate. Refrigerate until firm but not solid, about 1½ hours.

Line a rimmed baking sheet with parchment paper. Using a 1-inch spring-loaded scoop, scoop chocolate mixture into balls, and place on prepared pan. Freeze until set, about 15 minutes.

Using your hands, roll balls to smooth edges. Roll in coconut. Cover and refrigerate for up to 10 days. Let stand at room temperature for 10 minutes before serving.

MAKES ABOUT

- 1 (11-ounce) bag white chocolate morsels
- 10 tablespoons unsalted butter, cubed
- 6 tablespoons heavy whipping cream
- ½ cup toasted pecans, finely chopped
- ½ cup finely chopped dried pineapple
- 1½ cups sweetened flaked coconut

Chocolate-Bourbon Truffles

In a medium microwave-safe bowl, combine chocolate morsels, cream, and butter. Microwave on medium in 1-minute intervals, stirring between each, until almost melted (about 2 minutes and 15 seconds total). Whisk until mixture is completely smooth. Whisk in bourbon and vanilla. Pour into a 9-inch pie plate. Refrigerate until firm but not solid, about 1½ hours.

Line a large baking sheet with parchment paper. Using a 1-inch spring-loaded ice cream scoop, scoop chocolate mixture into balls, and place on prepared pan. Freeze until set, about 15 minutes.

Using your hands, roll balls to smooth edges. Roll in pecans. Cover and refrigerate for up to 10 days. Let stand at room temperature for 10 minutes before serving.

MAKES ABOUT 30

- 1 cup bittersweet chocolate morsels
- 1 cup semisweet chocolate morsels
- ¾ cup heavy whipping cream
- 1 tablespoon unsalted butter
- 3 tablespoons bourbon
- ½ teaspoon vanilla extract
- 2 cups toasted pecans, chopped

Salted Caramel and Cashew Truffles

MAKES ABOUT 48

2 cups sugar
½ cup water
¼ cup light corn syrup
½ cup unsalted butter
1 cup heavy whipping
  cream
1 cup chopped salted
  cashews
1 teaspoon sea salt
6 (4-ounce) bars
  bittersweet chocolate,
  chopped and divided
Garnish: sea salt

In a large skillet, cook sugar, ½ cup water, and corn syrup over medium-high heat until mixture turns amber colored, about 8 minutes. Immediately remove from heat. Add butter, stirring until melted. Gradually stir in cream until mixture is smooth. Stir in cashews and salt. Add 8 ounces chopped chocolate, and stir until chocolate is melted. Spoon mixture into a 13x9-inch baking dish. Cover and refrigerate until firm, about 8 hours.

Line a baking sheet with parchment paper. Roll caramel mixture into 1-inch balls, and place on prepared pan. Freeze for 1 hour.

In the top of a double boiler, place remaining 16 ounces chopped chocolate. Cook over simmering water, stirring occasionally, until chocolate is melted and smooth.

Using 2 forks, dip caramel balls in melted chocolate to coat, gently shaking off excess. Return to pan, and let stand until set. Sprinkle with sea salt, if desired. Refrigerate in airtight containers for up to 1 month.

Homemade
WITH LOVE

Homemade
WITH LOVE

Buttery Pumpkin Pie Fudge

Line a 13x9-inch baking pan with parchment paper, letting excess extend over sides of pan. Spray parchment with cooking spray.

In a large heavy saucepan, bring butter, sugars, evaporated milk, pumpkin, pumpkin pie spice, cinnamon, and nutmeg to a boil over medium heat. Cook, stirring constantly, until mixture registers 240° on a candy thermometer. Remove from heat; stir in white chocolate and vanilla until melted and smooth. Stir in pecans.

Pour mixture into prepared pan, and let cool completely. Using excess parchment as handles, remove fudge from pan, and cut into squares. Refrigerate in an airtight container for up to 5 days.

MAKES ABOUT 24 PIECES

¾ cup butter
2 cups granulated sugar
1 cup firmly packed
   brown sugar
⅔ cup evaporated milk
½ cup canned pumpkin
2 teaspoons pumpkin
   pie spice
½ teaspoon ground
   cinnamon
⅛ teaspoon ground
   nutmeg
1 (12-ounce) package
   white chocolate
   morsels
1½ teaspoons vanilla
   extract
1 cup chopped toasted
   pecans

Traditional Pralines

MAKES 24

1 cup firmly packed light
    brown sugar
1 cup granulated sugar
½ cup heavy whipping
    cream
¼ teaspoon baking soda
2 tablespoons unsalted
    butter
1 teaspoon vanilla
    extract
2 cups pecan halves

Line a baking sheet with parchment paper.

In a medium saucepan, bring sugars, cream, and baking soda to a boil over medium-high heat. Cook, stirring occasionally, until mixture registers 240° on a candy thermometer. Remove from heat; stir in butter and vanilla. Quickly add pecans, stirring vigorously until mixture thickens and loses some of its shine, 1 to 2 minutes.

Quickly spoon mixture by heaping tablespoonfuls, and drop onto prepared pan. (If mixture hardens, add 1 tablespoon hot water at a time until mixture returns to a spoonable consistency.)

Let cool until hardened, about 10 minutes. Store in an airtight container at room temperature for up to 1 week.

Shirley Temple Jelly Candy

Brush an 8-inch square baking pan with water.
In a small bowl, stir together gelatin and club soda. Let
stand until softened, about 5 minutes.

In a medium saucepan, combine ¾ cup sugar, cherry
syrup, lime juice, and corn syrup. Cook over medium
heat, stirring frequently, until sugar is dissolved, 3 to 4
minutes. Add gelatin mixture to sugar mixture, stirring
to dissolve. Pour into prepared pan. Let stand at room
temperature until set, 4 to 6 hours.

Using a sharp knife, cut candy into desired shapes. Just
before serving, toss in remaining 1 cup sugar. Store in an
airtight container at room temperature.

MAKES 24

½ cup unflavored gelatin
½ cup club soda, chilled
1¾ cups sugar, divided
⅔ cup maraschino
  cherry syrup
⅔ cup fresh lime juice
½ cup light corn syrup

Macadamia Fudge

2 cups sugar
¼ cup half-and-half
½ (4-ounce) bar unsweetened chocolate, chopped
2 tablespoons light corn syrup
¼ teaspoon kosher salt
2 tablespoons unsalted butter
½ teaspoon vanilla extract
½ cup toasted macadamia nuts, chopped

Line an 8x5-inch loaf pan with foil, letting excess extend over sides of pan. Spray with cooking spray.

In a medium saucepan, combine sugar, half-and-half, chocolate, corn syrup, and salt. Cook over medium heat, stirring occasionally, until sugar is dissolved and chocolate is melted. Cook, without stirring, until mixture registers 234° on a candy thermometer. Remove from heat; add butter and vanilla. (Do not stir.) Let stand until mixture registers 110° on a candy thermometer, about 50 minutes.

Stir until smooth and no longer glossy. (Mixture will be thick.) Spread mixture in prepared pan. Sprinkle with nuts, pressing lightly. Let cool until set. Using excess foil as handles, remove from pan, and cut into pieces. Store in an airtight container for up to 5 days.

Hummingbird Fudge

Line an 8x5-inch loaf pan with foil, letting excess extend over sides of pan. Spray with cooking spray.

In a large bowl, beat cream cheese with a mixer at medium speed until creamy. Add confectioners' sugar, vanilla, and salt, beating until combined. Gently fold in melted chocolate, pineapple, coconut, and banana chips. Spread mixture in an even layer in prepared pan. Sprinkle with pecans, pressing gently into top. Cover and refrigerate until firm, about 3 hours. Using excess foil as handles, remove fudge from pan, and cut into 1-inch pieces.

1 (8-ounce) package cream cheese, softened

3 cups confectioners' sugar

½ teaspoon vanilla extract

¼ teaspoon salt

3 (4-ounce) bars white chocolate, melted

¾ cup chopped dried pineapple

½ cup sweetened flaked coconut, toasted

½ cup chopped banana chips

⅔ cup toasted pecans, chopped

Cookie Butter Fudge

MAKES ABOUT 25 PIECES

2½ cups sugar
1 cup marshmallow crème*
¾ cup evaporated milk
¼ cup unsalted butter
½ teaspoon kosher salt
1 cup creamy cookie butter*
¼ teaspoon apple pie spice
½ cup toasted slivered almonds, chopped

Line an 8-inch square baking pan with foil, letting excess extend over sides of pan; spray with cooking spray.

In a large heavy saucepan, combine sugar, marshmallow crème, evaporated milk, butter, and salt. Cook over medium-low heat, whisking occasionally, until smooth, about 10 minutes. Bring to a boil over medium heat, stirring frequently, about 10 minutes. Cook, stirring constantly to prevent scorching, until mixture begins to turn light brown, about 6 minutes. Remove from heat.

Add cookie butter and apple pie spice, stirring until smooth. Pour mixture into prepared pan, spreading to edges. Sprinkle with almonds. Let cool completely on a wire rack. Using excess foil as handles, remove from pan, and cut into pieces.

We used Kraft Jet-Puffed Marshmallow Crème and Biscoff Cookie Butter.

Chocolate Peanut Butter Fudge

Line an 8-inch square baking pan with foil, letting excess extend over sides of pan. Spray with cooking spray.

In a medium heavy-bottomed saucepan, bring sugar, butter, and evaporated milk to a boil over medium heat. Cook, stirring occasionally, until mixture registers 238° on a candy thermometer. Remove from heat, and stir in peanut butter morsels, marshmallow crème, and vanilla until melted and smooth. Spread mixture into prepared pan. Let cool for 30 minutes.

In a small saucepan, heat cream over medium-low heat just until bubbles form around sides of pan. Remove from heat, and stir in chocolate until melted and smooth. Gently spread onto peanut butter layer. Let cool for 10 minutes. Cover and refrigerate until firm and set, about 4 hours.

Using excess foil as handles, remove from pan, and cut into 1½-inch pieces. Refrigerate in an airtight container for up to 5 days.

MAKES ABOUT 36 PIECES

1 cup sugar
¾ cup butter
¾ cup evaporated milk
1½ cups peanut butter morsels
1 (7-ounce) jar marshmallow crème
½ teaspoon vanilla extract
⅓ cup heavy whipping cream
1 cup semisweet chocolate morsels

Marshmallow Macadamia Fudge

MAKES ABOUT 12 PIECES

2½ cups sugar
1 (7.5-ounce) jar
   marshmallow crème
⅔ cup evaporated milk
¼ cup unsalted butter
½ teaspoon salt
1 (11-ounce) bag white
   chocolate morsels
1½ cups chopped
   macadamia nuts,
   divided
1 cup miniature
   marshmallows

Line a 9-inch square baking pan with foil, letting excess extend over sides of pan.

In a medium saucepan, cook sugar, marshmallow crème, milk, butter, and salt over medium heat until melted. Bring to a simmer, and cook for 5 minutes. Add white chocolate and 1 cup macadamia nuts. Stir until chocolate is melted. Pour into prepared pan. Top with marshmallows and remaining ½ cup nuts. Let cool until firm, about 2 hours. Using excess foil as handles, remove from pan, and cut into 1½-inch squares.

Turtle Fudge

Line a 9-inch square baking pan with foil, letting excess extend over sides of pan.

In a large saucepan, combine sugar, milk, and shortening. Cook over high heat, stirring constantly, until mixture registers 234° on a candy thermometer, about 4 minutes. Remove from heat; add chocolates, marshmallow crème, vanilla, and ¾ teaspoon salt, stirring until smooth. Fold in candies. Spread into prepared pan. Top with pecans and remaining ¼ teaspoon salt. Let cool completely.

Using excess foil as handles, remove from pan, and cut into small squares. Store in an airtight container for up to 5 days.

We used Rolos.

MAKES ABOUT 36

- 2¾ cups sugar
- ¾ cup whole milk
- ¾ cup butter-flavored shortening
- 2 (4-ounce) bars semisweet chocolate, chopped
- 1 (4-ounce) bar unsweetened chocolate, chopped
- 1 (7-ounce) jar marshmallow crème
- 2 teaspoons vanilla extract
- 1 teaspoon sea salt, divided
- 28 chocolate-covered caramel candies,* halved
- 1 cup chopped toasted pecans

Chocolate Peppermint Marshmallows

3 (0.25-ounce)
   envelopes unflavored
   gelatin
1 cup water, divided
1½ cups granulated
   sugar
1 cup light corn syrup
¼ teaspoon kosher salt
1 teaspoon vanilla
   extract
½ cup plus 2 teaspoons
   unsweetened cocoa
   powder, divided
⅓ cup confectioners'
   sugar
⅓ cup cornstarch
2 (4-ounce) bars
   semisweet chocolate,
   chopped
¼ cup peppermints,
   crushed

Spray an 11x7-inch baking dish with cooking spray. Spray a spatula with cooking spray.

In a small microwave-safe bowl, stir together gelatin and ½ cup water. Let stand until softened, about 5 minutes.

In a medium saucepan, stir together granulated sugar, corn syrup, salt, and remaining ½ cup water until moistened; bring to a boil over medium-high heat, stirring occasionally. Cook, without stirring, until mixture registers 250° on a candy thermometer. Pour mixture into the bowl of a stand mixer fitted with the whisk attachment, and let cool until a candy thermometer registers 210°. Beat at low speed for 1 minute.

Microwave gelatin mixture on high until dissolved, about 10 seconds. Gradually add gelatin mixture and vanilla to sugar mixture, beating just until combined. Increase mixer speed to high, and beat for 5 minutes. Reduce mixer speed to medium, and gradually add ½ cup cocoa, beating until combined. Spread mixture into prepared pan with sprayed spatula, smoothing top. Let stand at room temperature for 2 hours.

Sift together confectioners' sugar, cornstarch, and remaining 2 teaspoons cocoa onto a rimmed baking sheet. Turn out marshmallow onto sugar mixture. Using kitchen scissors coated in sugar mixture, cut marshmallows into 2 ½-inch squares. Dredge marshmallows in sugar mixture, shaking off excess; place on a wire rack.

In a small microwave-safe bowl, heat chocolate on high in 15-second intervals, stirring between each, until melted and smooth. Dip marshmallows halfway into melted chocolate, and sprinkle with peppermints. Return to wire rack, and let stand until chocolate is set, about 2 hours. Store in an airtight container for up to 3 days.

Chocolate-Filled Meringue Kisses

Preheat oven to 200°. Line baking sheets with parchment paper.

Place jumbo chocolate morsels at least 2 inches apart on prepared pans.

In the top of a double boiler, whisk together egg whites, sugar, raspberry extract, and cream of tartar. Cook over simmering water, whisking constantly, until mixture registers 140° on a candy thermometer. Remove from heat. Immediately pour mixture into the bowl of a stand mixer fitted with the whisk attachment; beat at high speed until stiff glossy peaks form, about 3 minutes. Add desired amount of food coloring, stirring to combine.

Place mixture in a pastry bag fitted with a star tip. Pipe meringues onto chocolate morsels to cover completely.

Bake for 2 hours. Turn oven off, and let meringues stand in oven with door closed for 2 hours. Store in airtight containers at room temperature for up to 1 week.

MAKES 36

36 jumbo chocolate
   morsels
3 egg whites, room
   temperature
1 cup sugar
½ teaspoon raspberry
   extract
¼ teaspoon cream
   of tartar
Red liquid food coloring

Kitchen TIP

Don't use your stand mixer bowl on top of your double boiler. It will take a longer time for the mixture to form stiff glossy peaks.

Peppermint Meringue Kisses

1 cup peppermint
   candies (about 30
   peppermints)
2 large egg whites, room
   temperature
½ teaspoon cream of
   tartar
⅔ cup superfine sugar,
   divided
1 teaspoon vanilla
   extract

Preheat oven to 350°. Line 2 baking sheets with parchment paper.

In the work bowl of a food processor, place peppermint candies; pulse until finely chopped. Set aside.

In the bowl of a stand mixer fitted with the whisk attachment, beat egg whites at high speed until foamy, about 1 minute. Add cream of tartar, and beat until fluffy but not dry. (Do not overbeat.) Add ⅓ cup sugar, 3 tablespoons at a time, beating until combined. Beat in vanilla. Add remaining ⅓ cup sugar, 3 tablespoons at a time, beating until mixture is glossy and sugar is dissolved, about 6 minutes. Gently fold in crushed peppermints.

Spoon meringue into a piping bag fitted with a round tip. Pipe meringue onto prepared pans in 1-inch circles, leaving a point at the top to make a "kiss" shape.

Place pans in preheated oven, and turn oven off. Let meringues stand in oven with door closed until crisp and dry, at least 2 hours or overnight.

Chocolate-Dipped Almond Meringues

Preheat oven to 250°. Line a baking sheet with parchment paper. (See Kitchen Tip.)

In a large bowl, beat egg whites, cream of tartar, and salt with a mixer at medium speed until foamy. Increase mixer speed to high. Gradually add sugar, beating until stiff peaks form. Beat in almond extract. Using a 2-teaspoon scoop, drop meringue 2 inches apart onto prepared pan.

Bake until meringues feel dry to the touch and can be lifted from parchment paper, about 1 hour and 15 minutes. Turn oven off, and let meringues stand in oven with door closed until centers are dry, about 1½ hours. Remove from oven, and let cool completely, about 30 minutes.

Place a sheet of wax paper on a work surface. Dip meringues halfway in melted chocolate, scraping excess on edge of bowl. Place on wax paper. Sprinkle with almonds. Let stand in a cool place (do not refrigerate) until chocolate is set and meringues can be easily removed from wax paper, about 2 hours. Store in an airtight container for up to 5 days.

Kitchen TIP

To keep parchment paper from sliding, place several dots of meringue, about ½ teaspoon each, around edges and center of baking sheet. Place parchment paper over meringue, pressing gently to adhere.

MAKES ABOUT 24

2 large egg whites, room temperature
¼ teaspoon cream of tartar
⅛ teaspoon kosher salt
½ cup sugar
¼ teaspoon almond extract
6 ounces semisweet chocolate, melted
½ cup sliced almonds, toasted and coarsely chopped

Pink Cotton Candy Macarons

Makes 50

2½ cups confectioners'
  sugar
2½ cups almond flour
6 large egg whites, room
  temperature and
  divided
Pink food coloring paste
1 cup granulated sugar
¼ cup water
⅛ teaspoon egg white
  powder
1 teaspoon raspberry
  extract
White Chocolate
  Ganache (recipe
  follows)

WHITE CHOCOLATE GANACHE
Makes 1¼ cups

¾ cup heavy whipping
cream
2 cups white chocolate
morsels

In the work bowl of a food processor, process confectioners' sugar and flour until finely ground. In a large bowl, beat flour mixture and 3 egg whites with a mixer at medium speed until combined. Beat in desired amount of food coloring.

In a small saucepan, heat granulated sugar and ¼ cup water over medium heat until mixture registers 240° on a candy thermometer.

In the bowl of a stand mixer fitted with the whisk attachment, beat egg white powder and remaining 3 egg whites at high speed until soft peaks form. With mixer on medium speed, slowly add hot syrup to egg whites, beating until meringue has thickened and cooled, about 3 minutes. Beat in raspberry extract. Fold meringue into almond mixture with a spatula, a little at a time, until combined and batter is loose.

Preheat oven to 270°. Lined several rimmed baking sheets with parchment paper. Using a pencil, draw 1½-inch circles 2 inches apart onto parchment; turn parchment over. Place batter in a pastry bag fitted with a medium round tip. Pipe batter onto drawn circles on prepared pans. Drop pans on counter several times to release air bubbles. Let stand for 20 minutes.

Bake until firm to the touch, 17 to 20 minutes. Let cool completely. Wrap in plastic wrap, and refrigerate overnight in an airtight container.

Place White Chocolate Ganache in a pastry bag fitted with a medium round tip. Pipe filling onto flat side of half of macarons. Place remaining macarons, flat side down, on top of filling.

WHITE CHOCOLATE GANACHE
In a medium saucepan, heat cream over medium-high heat until simmering but not boiling. Remove from heat; add chocolate, whisking until melted and smooth. Refrigerate in an airtight container overnight.

Toasted Pecan-Topped Divinity

Line rimmed baking sheets with wax paper; lightly spray paper with cooking spray. Spray 2 spoons with cooking spray.

In a large heavy-bottomed stainless steel saucepan, stir together sugar, corn syrup, ½ cup water, and salt just until moistened. Cook over medium heat, without stirring, until mixture registers 258° on a candy thermometer, about 18 minutes. As needed, brush sides of saucepan with a pastry brush dipped in water to prevent sugar crystals from forming.

Meanwhile, in the bowl of a stand mixer fitted with the whisk attachment, beat egg whites at medium speed until foamy. With mixer on high speed, add cream of tartar, beating until stiff peaks form. With mixer running, carefully pour hot sugar mixture into egg whites in a thin, steady stream. Add vanilla, and beat until mixture holds its shape and begins to lose its shine, 5 to 9 minutes.

Working quickly using the sprayed spoons, drop mixture by rounded tablespoonfuls onto prepared pans, and top each with a pecan half. Let stand until mounds are dry and can easily be removed from paper, about 6 hours. Store in an airtight container for up to 2 days.

MAKES ABOUT 24

2½ cups sugar
½ cup light corn syrup
½ cup water
¼ teaspoon salt
2 large egg whites, room temperature
¼ teaspoon cream of tartar
1½ teaspoons vanilla extract
Toasted pecan halves

Sweet Treats

MAKE-AND-TAKE RECIPES STAR AT
A PICNIC OR HOLIDAY GATHERING
AND QUICKLY BECOME FAVORITES
FOR YEARS TO COME.

French Vanilla Coffee Mousse

**3 cups heavy whipping
cream, divided**
**2 tablespoons ground
French vanilla–
flavored coffee**
**1½ cups chopped
semisweet chocolate**
**1 (3-ounce) bar milk
chocolate, chopped**
**½ teaspoon vanilla
extract**
¾ cup granulated sugar
**Garnish: fresh
raspberries, fresh
mint leaves,
confectioners sugar**

In a medium saucepan, bring 1 cup cream and coffee to a boil over medium-high heat; remove from heat.

In a medium bowl, combine chocolates. Strain cream mixture through a fine-mesh sieve over chocolates; stir until chocolates are melted.

In a medium bowl, beat vanilla and remaining 2 cups cream with a mixer at high speed until soft peaks form. Gradually add granulated sugar, beating until stiff peaks form. Fold whipped cream mixture into chocolate mixture. Cover and refrigerate until chilled. Garnish with raspberries, mint, and confectioners' sugar, if desired.

Banana Baklava with Toffee Drizzle

Preheat oven to 350°. Spray a 13x9-inch baking dish with baking spray with flour.

In a large skillet, melt ½ cup butter over medium heat. Add brown sugar, condensed milk, corn syrup, and vanilla, stirring to combine. Cook for 10 minutes, stirring occasionally. Remove from heat.

In a microwave-safe dish, place remaining 1 cup butter. Microwave on high in 30-second intervals, stirring between each, until melted.

Place 1 sheet phyllo in bottom of prepared pan. Brush with melted butter. Repeat procedure with phyllo and melted butter 5 times. Spread 1 cup toffee sauce over phyllo; sprinkle with walnuts and top with banana slices.

Place 1 sheet phyllo over bananas. Brush with melted butter. Continue layering phyllo, brushing with melted butter between each sheet. Brush top with melted butter.

Bake until golden brown, 20 to 25 minutes. Pour remaining toffee sauce over baklava immediately after removing from oven. Let cool completely before serving.

MAKES ABOUT 15 SERVINGS

- 1½ cups unsalted butter, divided
- 2 cups firmly packed brown sugar
- 1 (14-ounce) can sweetened condensed milk
- ½ cup light corn syrup
- 1 teaspoon vanilla extract
- ½ (16-ounce) package frozen phyllo dough, thawed
- ½ cup finely chopped walnuts
- 2 bananas, sliced

Miniature Pavlovas

1 cup sugar
¼ teaspoon cream of
   tartar
3 large egg whites
1 teaspoon vanilla
   extract
1 (3.4-ounce) box white
   chocolate instant
   pudding mix
2 cups milk
1 tablespoon amaretto
Garnish: fresh
   pomegranate arils,
   fresh mint

Preheat oven to 250°. Line baking sheets with parchment paper.

In a small bowl, whisk together sugar and cream of tartar.

In the top of a double boiler, combine sugar mixture, egg whites, and vanilla. Cook over simmering water, whisking constantly, until mixture registers 140° on a candy thermometer. Remove from heat. Immediately pour mixture into the bowl of a stand mixer fitted with the whisk attachment; beat at high speed until glossy stiff peaks form, 8 to 10 minutes.

Place meringue in large pastry bag fitted with a large round tip. Pipe meringue into 2-inch mounds on prepared pans. Using the back of a spoon, make wells in center of meringues.

Bake until hard and dry, about 1 hour and 15 minutes. Turn oven off, and let meringues stand in oven with door closed overnight.

In a medium bowl, whisk together pudding mix, milk, and amaretto until smooth. Refrigerate for 5 minutes. Spoon pudding into meringues. Garnish with pomegranate arils and mint, if desired. Serve immediately.

Chocolate-Topped Cheesecake Bars

Preheat oven to 350°. Line a 13x9-inch baking pan with parchment paper. Spray with baking spray with flour.

In a medium bowl, stir together crushed graham crackers, melted butter, and salt until combined. Firmly press mixture into bottom of prepared pan.

Bake until golden brown, about 12 minutes. Let cool completely. Reduce oven temperature to 275°.

In the bowl of a stand mixer fitted with the paddle attachment, beat cream cheese and sugar at medium speed until smooth. Add flour, beating to combine. Add eggs, one at a time, beating well after each addition. Add sour cream, milk, and vanilla, beating until smooth. Pour batter onto prepared crust.

Bake until center is set, about 45 minutes. Turn oven off, and leave cheesecake in oven with door closed for 45 minutes. Remove from oven, and let cool completely.

In a small saucepan, heat cream just to a boil. Remove from heat, and stir in chocolate until melted and smooth. Let cool for 15 minutes. Pour over cheesecake. Refrigerate until cooled and set, at least 4 hours. Using a sharp knife, cut into bars. Garnish with Sugared Rose Petals, if desired.

SUGARED ROSE PETALS
In a small bowl, whisk together egg white powder and 2 tablespoons water until smooth. Using a paintbrush, brush egg white mixture onto rose petals. Dip petals in sugar to coat. Place sugared petals on a sheet of parchment paper. Let dry overnight before using.

NOTE: Sugared Rose Petals can be made up to 4 days in advance; store in an airtight container at room temperature.

MAKES 16

- **2½ cups crushed cinnamon graham crackers**
- **½ cup unsalted butter, melted**
- **½ teaspoon kosher salt**
- **3 (8-ounce) packages cream cheese, softened**
- **1 cup sugar**
- **3 tablespoons all-purpose flour**
- **3 large eggs**
- **1 (8-ounce) container sour cream**
- **2 tablespoons whole milk**
- **2 teaspoons vanilla extract**
- **2 cups heavy whipping cream**
- **2 cups semisweet chocolate morsels**
- **Garnish: Sugared Rose Petals (recipe follows)**

SUGARED ROSE PETALS
MAKES 2 CUPS

- **2 teaspoons egg white powder**
- **2 tablespoons water**
- **2 cups organic rose petals**
- **1 cup sugar**

Mini Cheesecakes with Salted Caramel Sauce

2¼ cups graham cracker
  crumbs
½ cup unsalted butter,
  melted
¼ cup firmly packed light
  brown sugar
2 teaspoons ground
  cinnamon
4 (8-ounce) packages
  cream cheese, softened
1 cup granulated sugar
3 tablespoons heavy
  whipping cream
1 teaspoon vanilla extract
4 large eggs
Salted Caramel Sauce
  (recipe follows)

SALTED CARAMEL SAUCE
MAKES 1 CUP

1 cup firmly packed light
  brown sugar
½ cup heavy whipping
  cream
¼ cup unsalted butter
1 cup pecan halves
2 teaspoons vanilla
  extract
1 teaspoon sea salt

Preheat oven to 350°. Line a 13x9-inch baking pan with foil, letting excess extend over sides of pan.

In a medium bowl, stir together graham cracker crumbs, melted butter, brown sugar, and cinnamon until combined. Press mixture into bottom of prepared pan.

Bake for 10 minutes; let cool.

In a large bowl, beat cream cheese, granulated sugar, cream, and vanilla with a mixer at medium speed until creamy. Add eggs, one at a time, beating just until combined after each addition. Pour cream cheese mixture over prepared crust.

Place baking pan in a roasting pan. Fill roasting pan with enough water to come halfway up sides of baking pan.

Bake until center is set, about 20 minutes. Let cool completely on a wire rack. Cover and refrigerate for at least 4 hours or up to 3 days. Using excess foil as handles, gently remove cheesecake from pan, and cut into squares. Top with Salted Caramel Sauce.

SALTED CARAMEL SAUCE
In a small saucepan, cook brown sugar, cream, and butter over medium-low heat, whisking frequently, until thickened, about 10 minutes. Remove from heat; stir in pecans, vanilla, and salt. Let cool for 10 minutes before serving.

White Chocolate Pecan Brittle

Generously spray a rimmed baking sheet with cooking spray.

In a large saucepan, bring sugar, corn syrup, ⅓ cup water, and salt to a boil over medium-high heat, stirring just until sugar is dissolved. Reduce heat to medium; cook until mixture registers 250° on a candy thermometer. Stir in pecans; cook, stirring occasionally to avoid scorching, until mixture registers 300° on a candy thermometer.

Immediately remove from heat, and stir in butter, baking soda, and vanilla. Pour mixture onto prepared pan, spreading to desired thickness. Let cool completely before breaking into pieces. Drizzle melted white chocolate over cooled brittle. Store in a airtight containers for up to 3 days.

MAKES ABOUT 1½ POUNDS

- **1½ cups sugar**
- **1 cup light corn syrup**
- **⅓ cup water**
- **½ teaspoon salt**
- **1¾ cups coarsely chopped pecans**
- **3 tablespoons butter, cubed**
- **1 teaspoon baking soda**
- **¾ teaspoon vanilla extract**
- **Melted white chocolate**

Ginger Cashew Brittle

MAKES 10 TO 12 SERVINGS

2 cups sugar
1 cup light corn syrup
1 cup water
½ teaspoon salt
1 cup chopped salted
   cashews
¼ cup chopped
   crystallized ginger
2 tablespoons butter
2 teaspoons baking soda

Spray 2 large rimmed baking sheets with cooking spray.

In a large saucepan, cook sugar, corn syrup, and 1 cup water over medium heat, stirring frequently, until sugar is dissolved. Add salt; cook until mixture registers 250° on a candy thermometer. Add cashews and ginger; cook until mixture registers 290° on a candy thermometer.

Remove from heat; stir in butter and baking soda until frothy. Divide mixture between prepared pans. Let cool until hardened, 1 to 2 hours. Break brittle into pieces. Store in an airtight container for up to 5 days.

Orange-Spice Peanut Brittle

Grease a rimmed baking sheet, or line with a silicone baking mat.

In a heavy-bottomed saucepan, whisk together sugar, cane syrup, ½ cup cold water, and salt. Bring mixture to a boil over medium-high heat, stirring until sugar is dissolved. Cook, without stirring, until mixture registers 260° on a candy thermometer. Brush sides of pan with a pastry brush dipped in water to prevent crystals from forming.

Add peanuts; cook, stirring frequently to prevent nuts from burning, until mixture is light amber and nuts are light golden brown, about 5 minutes.

Remove from heat; add zest, butter, baking soda, red pepper, vanilla, and curry powder, stirring to combine (mixture will foam up vigorously). Immediately pour mixture onto prepared pan.

Using a greased spatula, quickly spread mixture in an even layer about ½ inch thick. Slip spatula under hot candy to loosen edges and bottom. Let cool for 1 hour. Break into large pieces. Store in an airtight container layered between sheets of wax paper at room temperature for up to 1 month.

MAKES 2 POUNDS

2 cups sugar
1 cup cane syrup
½ cup cold water
¼ teaspoon salt
2 cups roasted unsalted peanuts
3 tablespoons orange zest
1 tablespoon butter, softened
1 teaspoon baking soda
1 teaspoon crushed red pepper
1 teaspoon vanilla extract
½ teaspoon curry powder

Chocolate-Drizzled Honeycomb Candy

MAKES ABOUT 24 PIECES

1½ cups sugar
6 tablespoons water
2 tablespoons corn
   syrup
2 tablespoons honey
2 teaspoons baking soda
1 (4-ounce) bar
   semisweet chocolate,
   melted
Sea salt

Line a rimmed baking sheet with a silicone baking mat or foil.

In a large heavy-bottomed saucepan, stir together sugar, 6 tablespoons water, corn syrup, and honey. Bring mixture to a boil over medium-high heat (do not stir). Using a wet pastry brush, wash down sides of pan to prevent crystals from forming. Cook, without stirring, until caramel turns a light amber color and mixture registers 250° to 270° on a candy thermometer, swirling pan if necessary to prevent sugar mixture from scorching.

Remove from heat; add baking soda, whisking constantly until combined. Pour caramel mixture onto prepared pan. Let cool completely at room temperature.

Break cooled honeycomb into pieces. Drizzle with melted chocolate, and sprinkle with sea salt. Place honeycomb on parchment paper to let dry. Store in an airtight container at room temperature for up to 5 days.

White Chocolate Peppermint Bark

Line a rimmed baking sheet with parchment paper.

Melt white chocolate according to package directions. Spread in an even layer on prepared pan. Sprinkle with chopped bittersweet chocolate and crushed peppermint. Let stand until set. Break into pieces; cover and store for up to 2 weeks.

We used Baker's Brand Premium White Chocolate Baking Bars.

6 (4-ounce) bars white chocolate*
1 (4-ounce) bar bittersweet chocolate, coarsely chopped
½ cup crushed soft peppermint candy

Butterscotch Bark

3 (11-ounce) packages butterscotch morsels, divided

1 (12-ounce) package semisweet chocolate morsels

⅓ cup chopped roasted salted peanuts

¼ cup toffee bits

⅓ cup sweetened flaked coconut, toasted

Line a rimmed baking sheet with parchment paper.

Set aside ⅓ cup butterscotch for garnish. Melt remaining butterscotch and chocolate together according to butterscotch package directions. Spread in an even layer on prepared pan. Sprinkle with reserved ⅓ cup butterscotch, peanuts, and remaining ingredients. Let stand until set. Break into pieces; cover and store for up to 2 weeks.

Chocolate-Hazelnut and Butterscotch Bark

Line a rimmed baking sheet with foil.

In a medium bowl, stir together melted chocolate and chocolate-hazelnut spread until smooth. Pour chocolate mixture onto prepared pan; spread to about ¼-inch thickness.

Drop melted butterscotch by teaspoonfuls over chocolate mixture; gently swirl with the tip of a knife. Let stand in a cool, dry place until completely set, about 4 hours.

Break into pieces. Store in a cool, dry place for up to 1 week.

We used Nutella.

MAKES ABOUT 8 SERVINGS

2 cups bittersweet chocolate morsels, melted according to package directions
⅓ cup chocolate-hazelnut spread*
1 cup butterscotch morsels, melted according to package directions

White Chocolate Cranberry Toffee

54 saltine crackers
1 cup unsalted butter
1 cup firmly packed light brown sugar
1 (14-ounce) can sweetened condensed milk
1½ (4-ounce) bars white chocolate, finely chopped
1 cup chopped pecans
½ cup chopped sweetened dried cranberries

Preheat oven to 425°. Line a 15x10-inch jelly roll pan with foil; spray with cooking spray. Arrange saltines in an even layer on prepared pan.

In a medium saucepan, bring butter and brown sugar to a boil over medium-high heat; cook for 2 minutes. Remove from heat. Stir in condensed milk. Pour mixture over crackers.

Bake for 10 minutes. Sprinkle with white chocolate. Let stand for 1 to 2 minutes to soften. Using a small offset spatula, spread softened chocolate over baked crackers. Sprinkle with pecans and cranberries. Let cool completely. Break into cracker-size pieces. Store in an airtight container for up to 5 days.

Kitchen TIP

For a festive twist, swap out the pecans for chopped pistachios.

Butterscotch Haystacks

Line a baking sheet with parchment paper.

In a large microwave-safe bowl, combine butterscotch morsels and peanut butter. Microwave on high in 30-second intervals, stirring between each, until melted. Stir in chow mein noodles, pretzels, peanuts, coconut, and dried fruit.

Drop mixture by heaping tablespoonfuls onto prepared pan. Let cool for 45 minutes. Store in an airtight container for up to 5 days.

We used Sun Maid Fruit Bits.

MAKES ABOUT 24

1 cup butterscotch morsels
½ cup creamy peanut butter
1 cup chow mein noodles
1 cup thin pretzel rods, broken
½ cup salted peanuts
½ cup sweetened flaked coconut, toasted
½ cup chopped dried fruit*

Orange Zest Madeleines

1 cup all-purpose flour
⅔ cup granulated sugar
1 tablespoon orange zest
¼ teaspoon salt
2 large eggs, lightly
    beaten
½ cup unsalted butter,
    melted and cooled
1 tablespoon fresh
    orange juice
½ teaspoon vanilla
    extract
Confectioners' sugar

In a medium bowl, stir together flour, granulated sugar, zest, and salt. Add eggs, and beat with a wooden spoon until smooth. Add melted butter, stirring to combine. Add orange juice and vanilla, stirring to combine. Cover and refrigerate for at least 1 hour.

Preheat oven to 350°. Spray 2 madeleine pans with baking spray with flour. Spoon batter into prepared pans.

Bake until light golden brown, about 10 minutes. Let cool in pans for 2 minutes. Remove from pans, and let cool completely on wire racks. Sprinkle with confectioners' sugar. Store, covered, at room temperature for up to 3 days.

Mini S'mores Cups

Preheat oven to 350°. Spray a 24-cup mini muffin pan with cooking spray.

Press cookie dough squares into prepared muffin cups, making a well in center of each cup.

Bake until golden brown, 12 to 15 minutes. Let cool completely on a wire rack.

Place chocolate morsels in a medium heatproof bowl.

In a small saucepan, heat cream over medium heat, stirring frequently, just until bubbles form around edges of pan (do not boil). Pour hot cream over chocolate; cover and let rest for 2 minutes; stir until chocolate is melted and mixture is smooth. Let cool slightly.

Spoon or pipe mixture into cooled cookie cups, and refrigerate until set, about 1 hour.

In the bowl of a stand mixer fitted with the whisk attachment, beat egg whites at high speed until foamy. Add cream of tartar and vanilla, beating until combined. With mixer running, add sugar, 1 tablespoon at a time, beating until stiff peaks form.

Spoon meringue into a pastry bag fitted with a medium round tip. Pipe meringue onto ganache-filled cookie cups. Using a handheld kitchen torch, carefully brown meringue. Serve immediately.

MAKES ABOUT 24 CUPS

1 (16.5-ounce) package prescored sugar cookie dough squares
1 cup milk chocolate morsels
¼ cup heavy whipping cream
3 large egg whites
¼ teaspoon cream of tartar
½ teaspoon vanilla extract
¾ cup sugar

Sea-Salted Caramel Delights

1 cup prepared caramel topping*
2 sleeves buttery round crackers
1 (16-ounce) package chocolate-flavored candy coating, melted according to package directions
1 tablespoon sea salt

Spoon ½ teaspoon caramel onto one cracker; top with another cracker. Using 2 forks, dip into melted candy coating, covering completely. Place on a sheet of wax paper; sprinkle with sea salt. Repeat with all remaining ingredients.

Let stand for 1 hour. Store in an airtight container for up to 1 week.

*We used Smucker's Hot Caramel.

Salted Caramel Pecan Popcorn

Line a large rimmed baking sheet with parchment paper.

In a large Dutch oven, melt butter over medium heat. Add pecans and brown sugar; bring to a boil, and cook for 3 minutes. Stir in smoked salt and baking soda until combined. Remove from heat; gently stir in Dutch Oven Popcorn until coated.

Spread popcorn in an even layer on prepared pan. Let cool for 15 minutes.

DUTCH OVEN POPCORN

In a large cast-iron Dutch oven, heat oil over medium-high heat. Add popcorn; cover and shake until kernels begin to pop. Shake until popping slows to one pop every 5 seconds, 4 to 5 minutes.

MAKES ABOUT 12 CUPS

- ¾ cup unsalted butter
- 1½ cups pecan halves
- 1 cup firmly packed light brown sugar
- 1 teaspoon smoked salt
- ½ teaspoon baking soda
- Dutch Oven Popcorn (recipe follows)

DUTCH OVEN POPCORN
MAKES ABOUT 12 CUPS

- 1 tablespoon vegetable oil
- ½ cup popcorn kernels

Kitchen TIP

Continually shaking the pan while the popcorn cooks prevents burning and results in fewer unpopped kernels.

recipe index.